About the Author

Sydney has been writing poetry to help herself move through life since she was six years old. Writing has been her way to process anything that she feels stuck on, which happens a lot, more often than many may think. Sydney is always in the mood to watch a bad movie or listen to good music with her trusty companion, her cat Pancake. You can find Sydney on Instagram and TikTok, @SydneyXanth if you wish to keep tabs on her and her future endeavors.

The Past Few Years

Sydney Xanth

The Past Few Years

Olympia Publishers
London

www.olympiapublishers.com
OLYMPIA PAPERBACK EDITION

Copyright © Sydney Xanth 2023

The right of Sydney Xanth to be identified as author of
this work has been asserted in accordance with sections 77 and 78 of
the Copyright, Designs and Patents Act 1988.

All Rights Reserved

No reproduction, copy or transmission of this publication
may be made without written permission.
No paragraph of this publication may be reproduced,
copied or transmitted save with the written permission of the publisher,
or in accordance with the provisions
of the Copyright Act 1956 (as amended).

Any person who commits any unauthorised act in relation to
this publication may be liable to criminal
prosecution and civil claims for damage.

A CIP catalogue record for this title is
available from the British Library.

ISBN: 978-1-80439-523-3

This is a work of fiction.
Names, characters, places and incidents originate from the writer's
imagination. Any resemblance to actual persons, living or dead, is
purely coincidental.

First Published in 2023

Olympia Publishers
Tallis House
2 Tallis Street
London
EC4Y 0AB

Printed in Great Britain

Dedication

This collection is dedicated to the strongest ladies I know: Lori Entner, Nancy Dakin, and Wednesday Prendergast (a.k.a. my mom, grandma, and sister).

Acknowledgements

Tyler, my love, thank you for encouraging me to be strong, inspiring me with a love that I've never known, and being the person I always want to celebrate with. Mom, you have been my home and my guidepost for my entire life. Thank you for all of the sacrifices you made to make sure your kids could have the lives they dreamed of. Gramma, thank you for being my biggest cheerleader and for always reminding me how important it is to let people in so that I have a community to support me. Wednesday, my sister and best friend, thank you for always pushing me to be and do better. You're my rock, and I'm forever grateful to be able to call you my big sister. Dad and Angi, thank you for always having a home filled with love for me to run away to. A huge thank you to my best friends (you know who you are) for always believing I deserved my dreams to come true, and to my family not mentioned above for all the good stories that inspire me to keep writing. Love you all! Lastly, Pancake (my cat), thank you for saving me.

To Use When Ready:

i've got these walls up higher than you can jump,
it doesn't mean I don't want them to come crashing down.

i'm ready to start speaking what I want.

i want that dancing in our underwear in the middle of the
day kind of love.
a slow-burn, friends to lovers kind of thing young writers
will recreate time and again.

you know,
the kind that reminds you that your best friend is
the same person you'll be spending your life with.
the passion hidden in the comfort.

i want the headrush of knowing that when we're together
it will never be the last time.

i don't care about the hearts that came before mine,
so long as you give me yours.

i want to wake up to racing thoughts at 2am.
make a pancake feast for two.

you deserve to be celebrated every damn day.
i deserve to be celebrated every damn day.

so, let's party.

February 2019

i know it's expected
that after something really shitty happened to me
that i would become a shitty person.

i tried being bitter
petty
hateful.
i didn't like it.

instead,
while i am still hurt and healing,
i am taking the energy i would have put into becoming cold
and drawing light from it instead.

i've got so much love.

love for myself.
love for my family.
love for my friends.

something horrible happened to me.
i have been learning who is truly deserving of my love since.

studying the ways of self love.

i'm still angry.
still healing.

but I have seen the absolute worst of people
and it only made me more inclined to love.

Yellow, Part 2

here we are.
my yellow and myself.

he's still yellow.
i'm just not myself.

he's still living sunshine.
i'm just more cautious of the burn these days.

see, he never wants to hurt you.
but he will.
he says he cares and that you're never his second best.
but he won't walk his talk.

he's still yellow.
i'm just realizing that maybe I was never a fan of yellow for a reason.

i was born for the blaze of red.
born for the rolling tides of blue and the freedom of green.
i was not born to be caught in the spotlight of a yellow.

i still find it funny that he never really knew me.

all those long and deep talks,
i never spoke once of the day I stopped believing in love
(or the day i started to believe again).
i never told him of my strained relationship with forgiveness
after years of being stuck in cycles.

i want to blame him.
but what i said was true.

no one is at fault.
i couldn't let him in,
could only let him through.

here we are again.
he's still yellow.
i'm just done.

April 2019

they tell me to be patient.
things will be as they once were.
life will go back to the same numb vastness as before.

i will be the same girl again.
the same girl who fell in that trap.
the same lost girl without a home.
the same girl afraid to fight back.

i wish i could burn that girl to ashes.
wish that girl could die.

i think she did die.

they just want her back because it's what they're used to.
they're used to her being there.
used to her being careful and fragile.

they can't accept she died.

i am what is left of her.
i am the phoenix rising from her ashes.
i am powerful.

i warned them that things would change.
they tell me that these changes do not fit with the map of who i once was.
they are missing the point.

i am creating a whole new map for myself.
one that they will question with every step.

there is no longer time to play by their rules.
i am the cause of my own rebirth.

Sexual Assault Awareness Month

there have been studies done
proving that after trauma a brain can change.

i'm finding the small things are bigger now.

i ran into my best friend on sunday
and felt like i had to prove that i was okay.

as if showing signs of how much this really hurts
would somehow push those i love away from me.

damn.
this hurts.

i find myself dissociating a lot more again.
i say that i don't know why my brain is acting this way
to be reminded that i am going through my "a lot."

my "a lot" has made me change plans i was looking forward to.

sexual assault awareness month is ending,
but for those of us who have experienced sexual trauma,
we are always aware.

we are always reminded of what happened.
our brains are no longer what they were before.

we are different and we carry our trauma,
exhausted
because that's all we can do.

A Temple

this body is a temple.

the kind of temple that looks better after being ravaged by storms
and tagged by the best graffiti artists.

this body is a temple.

a temple that i alone control.
the kind of temple that is meant to continue to be used,
but only at my say-so.

this body is a temple.

i will use it to worship the sun beating down
and the water running clear.

this body is a temple.

a temple that was broken into once
and will never be the same again.

a temple marked by years of standing alone in the desert.

this body is a temple.
it's time i treat it as such.

this body is a temple
and i am the god above it.

Plans

begin with
"i had planned to never see my 20th birthday. i have made it to 25."

the middle will go something like:

i was always really good at making plans.
if i said i would be somewhere,
i would be there 15 minutes early.
you could count on me.
friends knew this.
family knew this.
they would ask me to be there at that time
and i would.

i was reliable.
i was great at keeping plans.

suddenly, i realized that my plans were not my own.

Notes

this body is no longer being preserved for viewing.
this body is ready to be used.

please take responsibility for the energy you brought into my life.

lost myself while pleasing others
to finding myself while losing the ones who said they
couldn't live without me.

Love in July 2019

just lying around.
thinking about how nice it must feel to fall in love.

not that i haven't been in love before,
because i have.

i just never fell into it.
to fall implies that you were caught.
but things don't play out like fairy tales
for the girls who learn from their dragons,
and leave their towers breathing fire.
it's not a fairy tale that i would want anyway.

i always caught myself in love.
it always happened with me crying and laughing at the same time,
so caught up in feelings that i couldn't speak out loud.

maybe someday i will find someone to say those words out loud to.
maybe someone who also breathes fire
and understands how refreshing it is to finally sit with a kindred soul.

two matching flames.

now that i've thought about it,
i don't want to fall in love.
i want to walk into love with someone worth my tears and laughter.

Trust

realized that i've become conditioned to believe
the things i enjoy are somehow wrong or just plain
ridiculous.
i apply this thought to everything i plan.

i like all those things that no one else does.
i talk about the things i enjoy,
and because they don't enjoy the same things
they will get annoyed and stop listening
instead of trying to understand why i like these things.

i was told that i cared too much
about the things that i enjoyed,
so i went to conventions and conferences alone.
i went to concerts alone.
i traveled across the country alone.

allowing myself to be alone
gave me the community i needed.

things have changed.
i'm working on keeping the community i found.

i find myself asking multiple times

if someone actually wants to go do that thing with me.
because i am expecting them to say that they have changed their minds.
when they say they are still in,
i am at a loss for words.

i am working on changing this.
i am learning to trust those around me.

my issues with trust are deep-rooted,
and i'm ready to dig them all up.

Respect.

tell me how to better show respect
to a man who never showed respect to my mother.
tell me how to respect a man
who never shows respect for the daughter standing in front
of him.
he told me to respect him.
i realized then that I don't know how.

i was still too young to know that love could die.
held onto my sister as the only fight i remember
was fought beyond her bedroom door.

i remember leaving.
i remember memories made without him,
whether he was living in the same town or states away.

he wants me to respect him,
but respect is not as easy as it seems.

i read old letters i wrote to him,
asking to be a bigger part of his life.
wanting so badly for a real relationship with this man.

watched from the sidelines as he coached a soccer team

for children not his own.

an online post let us know you got married.
you never let us in.

tell me how to respect this man.
teach me what respect looks like after 25 years of trying to connect.
please, show me how to move forward.
prove you want this to work now.

ask about the last few years.
a phone call let you know when i wanted to kill myself.
years later,
i called you myself to tell you that an evil man took what wasn't his
and i was working towards loving myself again.
you asked me one question: did i report?
i told you that i didn't, and you didn't ask why.
you never brought it up again.
the subject died.

i keep trying to strengthen the bridge between us.
now i wonder why i even try.

show me how respect works.
prove to me that you want to know who i am becoming.

don't beg for my respect.
stop asking for something you never cared to show.

walk the walk.

ask who i am becoming.
show interest in building a stronger bridge with me.
show me how to respect this man before me.
help me feel mutual respect.

this isn't a call out.
this is a call in.

to the man asking for my respect,
i'm not sorry for the ways you let me down.

i want to let go of the past hurts more than you could know,
so meet me in the middle.

to the man standing before me,
i still believe in the man you could be.

Numb

yeah, i'm numb.

we've been here before.
in the beginning i just wanted to feel something,
and pain was something i could control.

once i promised to leave that all in the past,
i sat in the numb.

i let the numb consume me.
didn't do a thing to stop it.
mom said she lost me.
i hope she doesn't think that now.

this time i just want to feel loved.
happy.
comfortable.

this time i'm looking only towards the good feelings.
i hope it shows.

i can reach for the warmth all i want.
it doesn't make the fog any less thick.
doesn't mean i'll actually feel something.

all it means is that i've tied a piece of me to those i love
and if they have hope for me,

i can't let them down.

September 2019

yesterday was hard.

i'm not talking about the kind of hard that made work difficult,
or made the thought of leaving the house too much to handle.

there was a shift of conversation at work.
someone said to imagine being held down and how it must feel.
i didn't have to imagine.

others mentioned the loss of control.
the complete terror that could come from that situation.
i knew the feelings well.

i was no longer at work.
i was back in that living room with his hand around my throat,
wishing for the pain to end.

i didn't tell anyone.
just came home and shut down my brain.

i don't know how to tell you about the flashbacks.
so i didn't.
but it happened.

i took a long hot shower.
scrubbed the memories off my skin last night.

i can breathe again.

Victim/Survivor

Perfect Victim:

played the part of the perfect victim.
kept her mouth shut.
buried what was done
deep down that she couldn't find it.
didn't tell a soul

… and then she did and the hurt came forth.

Perfect Survivor:

the idea of the perfect survivor.
a girl coming forward
repeating all the details for doctors, officers and lawyers.

****

she can scream from the rooftops what you did to her,
but only two people have heard her speak your name
attached to your crime.

she is neither the perfect victim nor the perfect survivor.
she doesn't need to be.

strong enough to stand in the middle,
unswayed by voices all around her.

she found out that just staying awake
is the easiest way to avoid the nightmares.
she no longer turns away
when she sees someone who reminds her of you.

therapist told her to build up some walls.
she's fine living raw.

if she can't trust the people she wants to keep in her life,
she'd rather not live at all.

she doesn't want to fight an endless war.
just wants to heal and feel free.
she just wants her own thoughts back.

so she'll stay straddled between
being the perfect victim and the perfect survivor.

Types

When you said she wasn't "your type"
She never told you that she didn't believe in types
and how if she did
you still wouldn't be hers.

October 2019

listening to a boy sing,
"we both lost me"
and isn't that the truth?

cause you were once sure of the broken girl with nothing left to lose
and i was once hoping you'd be the something that i might have to lose.

you said you're over this.
i feel you're over me.
i'm ready for the end.

i apologize too much.
you say that it's exhausting.
you don't talk for days.
you never want to make plans.
you snap too fast.
i fall back on eggshells.

what do you want me to do?
what am i fighting for?

you said you didn't scare easy.

but you don't care enough to ask why i do the things that seem to set you off.
you refuse to make a move.
i can't keep cutting off inches of myself to fit into the mold of what you say you need.

from the start you disguised yourself as a natural blue,
but you're just a sour red.
i'm scaring myself from dulling my color.

we both lost me.

Moments

i still have these moments
where my brain tells me that i am not deserving of the joy i
am feeling.

i have not worked hard enough on my recovery
to be feeling so vulnerable in someone else's arms.

these are lies.

i have worked nonstop.
i have found myself time and again
from the pieces others left me in.

i deserve joy,
but my brain still tells me that i do not.

i have not earned the right to joy
because they tell me that i am strong,
but i have yet to publicly name my rapist.

i have not earned the right to joy
because i am still unpacking childhood trauma that i never
let show.

i have not earned the right to joy
because it was never something i had to earn.

my joy was mine to take from the start,
i just never took the opportunity to reach for it.

i want to smile more.
to laugh more.
to love more.
i welcome joy into my life now.

Toxic

every time they talk she feels like she's on trial.
she swears she loves him,
though she doubts it's true.

this is getting exhausting.
she needs to heal.
she needs to breathe.

maybe one day the pieces will fit back together again,
but not today.

she's being accused of doing what he told her to.
they knew he needed to heal,
but what about her?

she refuses to be caught up in another toxic web.
every time he reaches out,
she's ripping open old wounds.

she swore she could love him,
but this isn't how love should make you feel.

(she never loved him)

November 2019

things need to stop.
or slow down.

my life has a way of getting bent
and folding over during the coming season.

holidays show up at the same time every year,
yet every year i surprise myself with how hard they hit
and the ways i react.

i want to scream.
I don't want to think about what happened 5 years ago,
or even 3 years ago at this time.
i don't want to talk about the reason i shut down and ran
away during this season last year.

i just want everything to calm down.
i want everyone to know i still love them,
but holidays aren't as light for me as they seem to be for all
of them.

i can't breathe when we gather together.
i arrive late on edge and leave early exhausted.
even when you promise no one expects anything more out

of me than my presence,
i know that comes with limits.

i can't say what's really on my mind.
i can't be the woman i am becoming around you.

i can't even explain why it hurts to be around you all at once.

Met a Boy

met a boy for a breakfast date
it all felt easy in a way i've never known

met a boy and he asked to kiss me.
he didn't just take like others before.
made warmth surge through my body.

met a boy and we walked together
talking about our lives and how we got here.

met a boy and it just felt right.
the ease of a natural green.

Every Time

because every time that something like this happens,
i have to blame the person in the mirror.

the person who i was.
the quiet girl who bent herself out of shape
to be what was expected.

because every time that something like this happens,
i regret all of the opportunities i said yes to.

i should have been there.
i promised i wouldn't leave and i did.

because every time that something like this happens,
it's impossible not to wonder how things could be.

i would have fought heaven and hell.

because every time that something like this happens,
i just want to run.

Quick to Heal

i couldn't write a poem about him.
felt as though i've said it all before.
another toxic tryst.

the hands of a narcissist found their way into my chest
to wring out what was left of my heart.

i couldn't write a poem about the boy who swore he loved me.
promised he would never hurt me.
yelled at me after saying things were over.
said he needed me.
but we both lost me.

i couldn't write a poem about how weak he made me feel.
or how strong i felt while walking away.

March 2020

this heartbeat isn't enough.
no, i need a sign
flashing overhead at all times
saying "i'm still here."

couldn't make good on any promise.
i'm ready now
to be a way out of hard times
telling you "i'm still here."

hoping this is coming out clear.
i've grown tired
staring down recovery
reminding myself "i'm still here."

April 2020

i couldn't tell anyone when it first happened because i knew
what would follow:
"what were you wearing?"
"a sheer black maxi skirt and a tank top."
"did you lead him on?"
"i don't know, i was just afraid."
i couldn't tell anyone, so i convinced myself it didn't happen.

there is a rapist in the president's chair.

even if i told someone, the message was clear: i would never
be believed.
let it eat away at me
losing myself a little more every day

when i finally shared what happened
it felt like the start of finding me
i was finally figuring this life out

now there's two rapists in contest for the president's chair

they are telling me that i will never be heard
my rapist is somewhere in my past
dead to me but better than me to the rest of the world

"choose a rapist" they say
"vote for the lesser rapist"
a rapist is a rapist is a rapist
they all blend together now

damn right, i'm angry
you've all shown your cards
i'll never be believed..

May 2020

this is the part
i become a burden
they tell me i am not

this is not my fault
what was done to me
was not my fault

two years
the same vicious things
repetitive torture

they say they want to know
i tell them that they do not
they do not need to carry this

they do not need the shame
the guilt that still lingers
these broken parts are all mine

this darkness is mine
you do not have to stay here
i can not escape

this is mine
i will push you away
afraid of the pain

two years of fighting
alone in the ring
past versus future

July 2020

i'll be the one to believe in you when no one else will.
rewriting my own dreams to make room for yours.

they said I was a dreamer
while stealing my innocence.
said I was a lover
while turning me cold.

i want what is mine.
is it yours?

i will love you more than i will ever love me.

let's repeat:
i will love you more than i will ever love me.

i will destroy myself time and again.

feeling stuck and there are thorns in my throat.

these choices are making me
and have made it seem the other way around.

what do I believe in now?

a compromise is just a creative way to say I broke another
promise to myself.

your past will always call you home,
while i leave mine in therapy sessions and long
conversations.

it's fine.
no, i'm okay.
i'll be fine.
always being second place just has a way about it.

wear me out.
like a wishing well,
i'm begging for change.

what happens next?

Lies I Told Myself

there always was a third person in this.
another heart once tied to yours.
still tied to yours.

she should have been the phantom.
left somewhere in the past.
when the cord between you was cut.

every day i fade more from view.
i'm the one on the outside.
looking into the land of the living.

a phantom visiting human emotions.
this wasn't built to last.
a shadow in the bed of a broken heart.

A Break in September 2020

i love him.
the way he knows me like no one else.
the way he always said the right words.
he always did the right things.

Temporary Goodbye in October 2020

my "i love you" came out as "goodbye"
not because i misspoke
but because i do love him.

i love the way he said what i was thinking
love the feeling of being in his arms
waking up next to him was a dream that didn't end

i love how he knows what he wants
even if it isn't what i want

my "i love you" was letting him go
not because i wanted to
but because he needed me to

he deserves his dreams coming true
deserves the future he's always imagined
one day i'll be able to say "i knew him when…"

he deserves the life he yearns for
even if i don't fit in it

my "i love you" came with the truth
ripped me open and raw
and i never even told him

Moments of Separation

she wore the shirt he gave her the other day.
it didn't feel like him the way it used to.
it only felt like a weight placed on her shoulders.
a reminder of everything they could have been.

she sat around her family that she's missed for some time.
wished he was there to help her hold it all together
when she missed his family more than she ever did hers.

going their separate ways may have been the right thing,
but it will never be the easy thing.

when that band comes on,
she skips to the next song.
the first band they sung along to together
will never sound the same to her ears again.

she wants to hear that he's doing better than she is.
wants his name to be on the next notification on her phone.
but the futures they are living for couldn't be more different.

some problems can't be compromised away.
sometimes love is not enough.
she wished love was enough.

When I Scared Myself With Missing You

maybe this should say
"missing you is making a mess of me"
but i know better
and i shouldn't leave an opening
locking all the doors and windows

stuck in a tower you placed me in
this pedestal is shaking from the storm
i have to jump before it crashes down

knowing i'll be the monster in your story
"why would she tear down all he built for her?"
people will say what they want
let them believe what they will
the truth is that i can't breathe any more

you would think being held so high
the air would be perfect up with the birds
you swear you will never hurt me
and ignore the pain all around us now

i can't be this for you
not meant to be a forever
i'm jumping from the highest tower

we all fall down sometimes

breaking all the old strings
promises i never should have made
every lie i ever told myself
did you really never notice
how i was always avoiding your potholes?

"missing you is making a mess of me"
and that's why i have to revolt

"missing you is making a mess of me"
turning me into the monster you can tell your next girl all about

Boundaries

boundaries should be seen as inviting
not intimidating.

i invite you to know
and love me in this way

not the way you suppose i should

Vices.

this is praying for a vice that doesn't lead to needing to be saved.
looking for a way to cope without ending 6 feet under.

always been an addict of whatever you can hide.
run away to find a purpose far from anywhere you've ever called home.

writing will find you in the final hour,
a new old hope to start again.

everybody knows you've been here before.
it'd be easier if they'd all just keep their mouths shut.

February 2021

spending days forgiving my survival self.

i've been curled up in the backseat,
gasping just to breathe.
watched the mile markers pass,
running out of gas heading
nowhere.

In Love

he says he holds onto the memory
when i said i loved him for the first time.
the look on my face
he'll never forget the way i blushed

i hold onto the moment
when he first asked for a kiss
the choice was mine
i've never forgotten the little things

before him love felt like:
jumping through missed hoops.
painting new masks every day.
something that was to be hidden

after him love feels like:
jumping on the bed.
painting flowers on a bad day.
something to be celebrated.

Not As Written

wrote about the love i wanted
the manic kind of love
that has you dancing in your underwear
in the middle of the day

thought up a love full of expectation
knowing no one could come close
a safety net of my own design

wrote about how
my heart was broken more by family
than any lover ever could
wrote about being alone

wrote about everything
but never what was real
never wrote what i needed

i needed a home
yearned to be found
to be kept by someone solid.

A Loss For Words in April 2021

i never had much practice
writing about good things

so when i try to write
about this love we share
it seems the words are lost

What I Want

taking some time
to get my head right
figuring me out
has been a waste

do i even want what i want
or is this all just expected?
will i let you all down
if i say what i'm feeling?

Torture

she's got her fingers grasped
tight around her lifeline
choking out her every breath
this shouldn't be so hard

saving herself was never easy
when she knew what evil
was stomping on her chest
holding her under water

what evil grabs her now
it's silent and invisible
she can't put a name to it
the darkness is ever changing

how can she defeat
what she doesn't even know?
she can't ask for help
while not able to explain.

May 2021 is for Healing

still young and fragile
still growing and healing

there are eggshells
all over this floor

there are landmines
all over her body

looking for some safety
searching for a way out

Lists.

pick apart this brain
leave traces on the floor
write letters to another self
imagine reasons to smile
find new ways to cope
remember to breathe
ask for help
lock the door
turn up the music
sing in your own key
scream to be heard
watch the old shows
feel something
anything

Me Again

i want to drive to the beach
ditch the phone
feel like myself again

want to start a revolution
even if i just change me
love myself again

want to run away
leave it all behind
find myself again

What Happened to Her?

i hate when people won't say the word
when they skirt over the trauma
like saying the word will hurt them

reminder that i am still here
(and hurting)
i'd say it more if you didn't flinch

the difference is it happened to me
i get the nightmares and flashbacks
the word doesn't hold power over me

you still won't say it
i haven't even told you details
the details would ruin you

(this is a warning before i say the word)
i was raped
and you won't even say the word.

Found.

can't help but wonder about all of the places she dropped pieces of herself,
and worry about the pieces that were taken from her.

she's lost track of what was left where.
who she was at the start is twice removed from who she is.
doesn't even know who she is.

what she wants is meaning.
she wants a reason for this pain that isn't phantom.

she wonders what would have happened if this and if that.
she thought she had something figured out
just to have it thrown away.

how can she trust the process now?

doesn't need to be saved,
she needs to be found.

What-Ifs

while the world of what-if seems perfect on paper
it's not a land i'd want to live in.

i don't believe everything happened for a reason
but i do believe in doing what is best.

i believe in taking the next best step
regardless of where you began.

getting stuck in the world of what-if is falling behind.

a girl once told me the clichéd
"the world is your oyster!
the word impossible even says i'm possible!"
and i have to ask:
what oyster gets stuck on the what-if?

We've All Been There

every time she takes notice
it's how you're being that better man
for another girl

it shouldn't even matter
just fucks her head even more
after your "cosmic love"

she doesn't hide a hope for some day
she's going through the motions
of moving on and letting go

Missing A BFF

i miss the way things were
when we would get into trouble
two best friends
the world was our playground

a weekend together
turned into tattoos and piercings
our mothers disappointed
in the good girls they raised

miss standing next to you
in the middle of the crowd
singing along
with all our favorite songs

remember your wedding day
joked his union was with us both
it's been years
of looking back

things are getting better
all i want is to share the good
with the one person
i can't seem to reach

this is just a long way
to say what needs to be said
after searching for you every day
i miss you more than anything

June 2021 Was For Them

knew a boy once who loved more than any other
he tucked flowers behind his ears
while singing all his favorite songs

he fell in love with a boy who'd rather stay in his own head
their love was something freeing
though no one else understood

the way they made a part of this world their own
grew a secret garden full of flowers
a place to be alone together

We Lost You

i heard you told the judge
that you had no connection
to family or to home

if i could go back
i'd change everything

never would have left
would have fought like hell
made them believe me when
i told them how she treated you

i would have stayed
all you had to do was ask

now home will never be the same
family doesn't mean the same
fuck

hating them for losing you
giving up before giving a chance
they took the wrong side years ago
ruined all of us in the end.

Strawberry Cupcakes

i've still got your recipe saved
the strawberry cupcakes you asked for
on some birthday years ago

don't think i'll ever use it again
should delete it from my home screen
it's only a reminder of some distant time
before everything got so messed up

some part of me still wishes
even after all these trials
that you'll come back some day
i'd bake your strawberry cupcakes again

it's all the wishing that hurts the most
they all let go some time ago
and they seem to be doing fine

Them.

could never hide the way he felt
when that boy looked his way
the deepest brown he'd ever seen
those eyes set him off

in search of something better
something that could stand his tests
it wasn't meant to be forever
but now a date is set

the invites have all been sent out
his heart locked on the man before him
forever may never be enough
for them it's just a start

It's Time

she came to me in a dream
telling me it's time for this crucible to end
there's no need to stay and suffer
but what if that's all i've ever known?

to love myself now i have to be selfish
but it's always been them first
their feelings always bigger in my mind
what if i can't find where to start?

there have been moments
when my life felt like my own
but those moments always fade away
what if this time is just as fleeting?

remind myself time and again
it's all right to fall and for my voice to shake
still so afraid to take that first step
what if i'm just made to be all but my own?

Crush

my first crush was the boy who lived next door
we created our own daring adventures
the world was always ours for the taking
though we never strayed far from home

there was also the boy that played kickball
he wrote his a's to look like sails on a boat
i never could find the courage to talk to him
but i still write my a's the same way he did

then came the girl that understood me
even though she spoke a different language
i never dared to speak of this crush so young
all i knew was what i didn't know

i didn't know how they'd react to me now
at an age that you'd shout about who you liked
i kept my mouth shut most of the time
easier to not say a thing than let them in

years passed and i never told a soul
constantly hid parts of myself to keep peace
i grew up and found my voice for a spell
came up with the words to come out

Villain/Survivor

we've got medusa in our corner.

stripped from our sanity and made to carry the burden.

blessed with a curse that keeps us safe from a distance.

call us your monster
while forgetting your own sin.

look in our eyes
you've turned yourself to stone.

you know how easy it is to flip a narrative
make a villain from a survivor.

don't say we made you look.

Still Missing BFF

there's something to be said
about the goodbyes that shatter worlds
the way they start something new
another chapter in this journey
pulling us miles and miles apart

i've got worlds within me
infinite chances to reinvent the girl you knew
never thought i'd live without you
years pass and i'm somebody else
still got marks from years with you

there's something to be said
about friendships ending in silence
ripping you to shreds without a word
thinking i wouldn't be who i am today
if it weren't for the months spent missing you.

Burn It Down

i can say i miss that place
and all your happy faces
but i miss me the most

no one seems to understand
i'm ready to burn all good things down
ready to scream and fight like hell

the fire is starting to show
getting angry too quickly
a short fuse just waiting to be lit

August 2021

it doesn't really make sense
to bring up the latest demon knocking on my door.

it's 3am again
i'm anything but fine.

some might say it's imposter syndrome
but years of therapy have taught me different.

i told you all what i wanted.
it was pushed aside.
laughed at like a bad joke.
said to be an over correction
after the world shattered over me.

i want so badly not to hurt a single one of you.
can't let you down after making you think i figured out an easier path.

easy isn't meant for me and you all know that.
you just don't want to admit
how i'm suffocating now.
refuse to see how i haven't been able to breathe.
when you tell me that how things are

is how they are meant to be
i'll bite my tongue and agree.

i've been doing it for you this whole time.
making a mess of me
ignoring the parts of me becoming louder every day.

you don't want to hear it.

i can't let you down.

you've given too much to get me here.

if i keep going i'll lose myself completely.

we're at a stalemate at 3am but it's all in my head.

Something Like A Swan Song

what i'm trying to say is:
you were my very first best friend.

i still carry love for you.
love for who you were.
love for who you became.

sadly,
i even carry love for the person i always expected you to be.

what i know is that i will always have fond memories of you.
even now that we are grown
i still dream of adventures with you.

a lot has changed,
but the kids we were will remain
forever unchanged in time.

i want to write something worthy of that friendship.

i want to write what could have been.

that is what i will do.

Peace in March 2022

i don't have to face this world alone.
haven't written in the longest time.
couldn't stand bringing up past traumas.
i faced them all alone.

got used to being the only one.
left with a mess in a busy airport.
hiding bruises under layers of makeup.
it was too easy being the solo one.

i guess i just needed someone.
to help me find myself again.
love me regardless of the scars.
glad to say i've found someone.

May 2022 & Healing

It's 4 years later
the nightmares of what happened still flash behind my
eyelids.

haven't written in the longest time.

i never wanted to be the writer
who hyperfixates on that one traumatic experience,

but fuck,
i have shit to say about what you did to me.

i get to be the crybaby you turned me into 4 years ago.
i am allowed to speak of what happened
while changing everything about me
so I'll never be the person you touched again.

had tarot cards read a while back
they said i still felt like I hadn't changed enough.

i haven't changed enough.

i still scrub my skin raw in the shower when the anniversary
comes

just to feel clean.
i still double check locks and keep most people at a distance so they don't have to know how guilty I feel on the worst days.

logically, my brain knows that i am not guilty
that i did all that i could.
logically, i know i am becoming stronger
have healed so much in such a short amount of time.

logic doesn't always have a home around here, though.

my body remembers it all.
this body carries memories of you that my brain has done all it can to forget.

this year when the anniversary came around
my body remembered first.
the pressure of you holding me down,
the exhaustion i felt for over a year after,
every single healed bruise you gave me was sore once again.

my brain finally caught up when the nightmares crashed my dreams.

found a therapist who's a perfect fit,
and she's got me processing my way to a life without your ghost.

it won't be easy, but i've got time.

found a partner who holds me on the darkest days,
encouraging my growth every day.
he's got a way of making me feel whole again.

i guess,
what i'm trying to say is that
i'm still here.

despite your best efforts,
you didn't ruin my life.

Raised Different

coming of age these days hits a little different

while all raised with faith
we learned the importance of hope
our brothers and sisters raised in fear
we learned to question
while they were learning to obey

their parents stumble
to make sense of a changed world
scared for the children
they only taught how to judge
in a new world that requires love

swear that they're not living in fear
while spreading lies that only hurt others
if the truth were to confront them
they wouldn't know the difference
their conspiracies have become religion

there's no hope living in constant fear
blind to the goodness all around them
the love taking root today
raising generations to be better

leaving their beliefs in the past

they are terrified they could have done better
raised their kids to ask questions
taught to love instead of judge
planted hope in the hearts of children
all the things we had and they had none.

If Only

here i am at 28.
feeling like 24 was a couple lifetimes ago.

only 4 years have passed.
i never thought i'd make it out alive.
one path after another.
i circled back.
could have let it end me.

can't let myself wander.
won't think of what-ifs.
don't want to die with if-onlys.

if only i fought back.
if only i said yes.
if only i didn't do what i did.
if only he didn't do what he did.

if only...

June 2022

this is when i admit
i found freedom before healing
and that has made all the difference.

Not Afraid

never wanted a fairy tale.
couldn't cut it as a princess.

i had my own dragon to fight.
my own moat to drown in.

iwas found by a knight though.
he made me want to make a home.

lost some friends along the way.
family thinned itself out.

i'm not afraid of being real.
just afraid of letting myself down.

i once wrote about how
i wanted to be like Sylvia.
wanted all of the figs on the tree
even those she could never reach.
want to do what she couldn't.

focused on my healing.
building the best version of me.

used to be scared of getting stuck.
now i know my home is in his arms.

once wrote about the love i wanted.
the love i thought i needed.
i didn't know myself back then.
was searching for something
that would only ever end me.

i know myself better now.
know who i am and what i need.

was always afraid of admitting how i felt.
with him, i'm not afraid any more.